Emily's Surprise

Story by Debbie Croft

Illustrations by Vicky Fieldhouse

"Are you going in to town this morning?"
Mum asked Dad, as he ate his breakfast.

"Yes, I am," said Dad.
"I need to buy some more food for the chickens.
And Bianca is coming with me.
I told her we would get those new shoes we talked about."

"What new shoes?" asked Bianca's younger sister, Emily.
"Can I go with Bianca
and get some new shoes, too, Mum?"

"No, Emily," said Mum, smiling.
"You can stay here with me today."

"But Bianca got new shoes at the start of the year," said Emily.
"And now she's getting more shoes! That's not fair!"

Before long, Dad and Bianca left to go to town
in the old farm truck,
and Emily stayed at home with Mum.

Emily was grumpy for the rest of the morning.
She had planned to ask her friend, Bella,
to come over to play.
But now she didn't want to. She was too upset.

"Mum, why is Bianca getting more new shoes?"
Emily asked, crossly.

"Emily, don't worry," said Mum, gently.
"Please stop asking questions.
You have some new scales to learn on the piano,
so why don't you go and practise them now?
Then, you can phone Bella
and ask her to come over for lunch."

Emily went into the family room
and sat down at the piano.
But she didn't feel like learning scales.
And she didn't feel like playing music.
She really didn't feel like doing anything.

Emily lay on the couch for a while,
thinking about Bianca.
She just couldn't understand why Bianca
was getting more new shoes.

After a while,
Emily heard the truck arrive back at the farm.
She walked out to the kitchen.

When Dad and Bianca came inside,
Emily could see how excited Bianca was.

"Mum, look at these!" said Bianca.

Mum looked inside the box Bianca was holding.
"Yes, those shoes look just right to me.
But they might need a bit of work to make them fit!"
said Mum, with a smile.

Emily was puzzled. She looked at Mum.
Then, she looked at Dad, and she looked at Bianca.

"Didn't you try on the shoes at the shop?" asked Emily.

"Well ... no, I didn't," said Bianca.
"Dad was in the shop last week,
and Mr Tibbs said he would make special shoes
that would be just the right fit!"

"Oh ..." said Emily.
"But why do you need special shoes, Bianca?"

“Come here, Emily,” Bianca said.
She opened the box
and unpacked four new horseshoes.

“Oh!” said Emily. “You tricked me, Bianca!
I thought Dad was buying you some *real* shoes!”

“They’re new shoes for your pony, Moonlight!
We wanted to surprise you,” said Bianca.
“Dad will put the shoes on Moonlight.
He knows how to do it.”

“You are a very good rider now, Emily,” said Mum,
“so we are taking you trail riding tomorrow.”

"Moonlight needs new shoes to walk over rocks that might be on the trail," said Bianca.

"Do you want to watch me put them on Moonlight this afternoon?" said Dad.
"You know I am good at putting shoes on horses."

"Oh, yes!" said Emily, happily.